Riccardo Nesti

THE CITIES OF ART

FLORENCE

History Art
Folklore

FLORENTIAE·CIVITAS

ATS Italia Editrice

Piazzale Michelangelo

Along the hills on the south side of Florence a wide avenue winds upwards between the cypress trees reaching the enormous Michelangelo Square with magnificent views of the city and surroundings. This immense "terrace" constructed in the last century by the architect Poggi dominates the entire valley of the Arno and Florence. Numerous small roads, silent and narrow, break off from the wide avenue and carry one back down between the olive groves into the city. There is, for example, the characteristic via San Leonardo from which one reaches the Forte di Belvedere, a 16th century fortress by Bernardo Buontalenti.

A Historical Outline

The history of the city begins in 59 B.C. when the Romans, under Caesar Augustus, founded the colony of "Florentia". The structure of this first urban "nucleus" was that of a Roman camp: a square 500 meters on each side formed by roads running parallel and perpendicular to each other. The central north-south and east-west roads ("cardus and decumanus") correspond respectively to the existing via Roma - via Calimala and the via degli Speziali - via Strozzi. The exact centre is the present Piazza Repubblica. The name "Firenze" derives from the Latin "florentia" meaning Flora and flower. Legend has it that the founders attributed such a name almost as if it were to promise a blossoming and growth for the population that had established itself in the fertile and flowering river valley. Little is known of the relationships or ties — if any — existing between the Roman community of Firenze and the pre-existing Etruscan community. The Etruscans had already settled throughout the north central part of the Italian peninsula as early as the 9th century B.C. and had given the name "Etruria" — translated in "Tuscia" by the Latins to the region of Tuscany (Toscana). In the first centuries of her history Florence suffered all the problems related to the propagation of Christianity — the development of a new religion and a new culture. In the second half of the third century St. John the Baptist

was declared the patron saint of Florence, substituting in importance — so to speak — the rule held by the pagan god Mars. In the same period lived Florence's first and only Christian martyr, San Miniato. In the year 393 the Bishop of Milan, Sant'Ambrogio, consecrated the first Christian church in the city: San Lorenzo. This was the time of the decline of the Roman empire of the West which fell under the pressure of the Barbarian invasions of 476. At this time the first delimitations of existent European nations were established as a result of the new domains founded by the barbarians in the ancient provinces of the Empire. Italy is also conquered territory; Florence was subdued first by the Byzantines in the 6th century, followed by the Lombards (7th-8th centuries) and finally the Franks (9th century). The struggle for survival superseded any pursuit or ambition for art and culture. The only exception was to be found in the monasteries; it is thanks to these institutions that the patrimony of Greek and Roman culture was conserved and protected. Under the reign of Charlemagne a new unification was established which guaranteed the stability necessary for renewed artistic and cultural productivity. Under his order construction was begun for the church of Santissimi Apostoli. It was later rebuilt in the 11th century. The period of Feudalism began with the death of Charlemagne and the consequent end of

San Marco Museum - Anonymous, 15th century - The Martyrdom of Savonarola - Detail

View from the Cathedral of Saint Mary of the Flower and of Palazzo Vecchio

the Carolingian Empire. This was determined by the breaking up and demarcating of territory into provinces or "feuds". The control of these was entrusted to feudal lords. The Empire itself, however, was reorganized and again unified in 962 under Ottone the First of Saxony. He joined together the reigns of Germany and Italy constituting the Holy Roman Empire. There ensued a very difficult period of contrast between papal power and imperial power that culminated in the excommunication in 1077 of Henry the Fourth by Pope Gregory the Seventh. In Florence this same contrast lead to a separation into coalitions, a disintegration of the city's unity. Preparing for battle, the people split into camps or zones within the city. The tower, which was originally conceived as a defensive structure, became the prevalent building in Florence. But only later was it also used as a dwelling. The city was encircled by a ring of walls within which one structures were built tightly up against one another. Extremely narrow streets twisted and turned — often seemingly without rhyme or reason. At the end of the 12th century a new form of social and political organization was established: the "comune". Typical characteristics of the "comune" are among others - as described at the time - "democratic participation in the management of city functions of public interest and a fundamental rule in the commercial and artisan activity in the economy of the city". The "arts" or guilds were created as a spontaneous and natural grouping together of workers based on mutual interest. The population increased notably, due above all to the migration of people from the surrounding countryside to the city proper. At this time the population of

Florence was estimated at about 100,000 inhabitants. It seems that the Wool Guild (the most important of the guilds) had about 30,000 dependents. By the first half of the 1200's the city extended beyond the other bank of the Arno river. Numerous bridges were built and a new and larger ring of walls was constructed. From the great commercial and economic expansion of this period arose an institution that was destined to characterize the economy of even modern nations: banking. In 1252 the first golden "florin" was minted. It become one of the most valued monies in Europe. Those years of great wealth and expansion were stained nevertheless with the blood of continued fraticidal wars. Sides were still taken according to the two great powers: those in favour of the Pope were called "Guelphs" — those in favour of the Emperor were called "Ghibellines". It is with the Guelph victory of 1289, however, that the Florentine republic finally found political stability. This naturally helped in the following years to concentrate all efforts on cultural and artistic activity. From 1295 to 1298 the architect Arnolfo di Cambio laid the foundations of the principal Florentine monuments: Santa Croce, Santa Maria del Fiore and Palazzo della Signoria. Together with earlier monumental structures (the Bargello, Santa Maria Novella), these still constitute today the highest expression in architecture. Consequently Florence became the indisputable centre of cultural life whose expression is manifest in the literary works of Boccaccio, Petrarch and especially Dante. Their works were already read and enjoyed throughout Italy during their lifetimes. Because the authors utilized the Florentine "tongue" instead of Latin — then the legitimate language for official documents and writings — Italian became the accepted language throughout the peninsula. It is for this reason that the great poet Dante is rightfully considered the father of the Italian language. The wealth and power of the economic expansion that has already been discussed began to concentrate in the hands of a few powerful families — giving place to a new kind of oligarchy. One name stands out among the powerful of the city, and its history was destined to be interlinked with that of Florence for centuries to come: Medici. Starting with Cosimo the Elder, the Medici took economic and political control of the city in the first half of the 15th century. Florence acquired a position of great importance in Europe on a commercial and especially financial level due to Cosimo's decisions at home. With his force of character and masterful management he succeded in consolidating Medici control of the city with the backing of the people. He also demonstrated his fine sensibility and intuition in his advice on cultural and artistic projects. In his merit is the great Church Council of 1439 brought from Ferrara to Florence. It is this Council which brought together for the last time the Churches of both East and West. This was an important occasion for the meeting of different cultures and especially for the revival of interest in classical civilization. The most important characteristics of the classical era are reflected in the works of the greatest artists of this period from Masaccio to Donatello. Beato Angelico to Filippo Lippi. Dating form this time are Donatello's bronze "David", Brunelleschi's magnificent dome of the Cathedral, Beato Angelico's frescoes decorating the convent of San Marco. Following Cosimo came his first son, Piero, and following him, Lawrence, called the "Magnificent" — Lorenzo il Magnifico. This title helps define the qualities or attributes of an exceptional man. The shrewd politician, the ardent and brilliant scholar gathered around himself the geniuses of the age. In Lorenzo's court lived philosophers as well as men of letters such as Agnolo Poliziano and Pico della Mirandola, artists such as Botticelli and Michelangelo. This is probably the most blissful and yet bittersweet moment in the history of the city; with the realization that time passes inexorably, there was an almost exasperated search for immediate pleasure. A kind of hedonistic lifestyle became the antidote for the melancholy provoked by this sense of the transiency of life. Then in 1492 Lorenzo died. His first son Piero followed but was exiled along with the rest of the family 2 years later. Charles the Eighth, King of France invaded the city and established a new Republic. These were the years of Savonarola, the Dominican priest and orator who became very popular fighting corruption and worldliness. He wanted to bring the Florentines back to a morality lost with the advent of humanism — lost with the rebirth of interest in the classical and "pagan" world. Two members of the Medici family in the 1500's became Popes: Leo the Tenth, son of Lorenzo il Magnifico, and Clement the Seventh, son of Giuliano, Lorenzo's brother who was murdered in the Pazzi family conspiracy of 1478. Clement the Seventh found in Charles the Fifth, Emperor of Spain, the perfect ally, enabling him to organize the return of the Medici family to Florence.

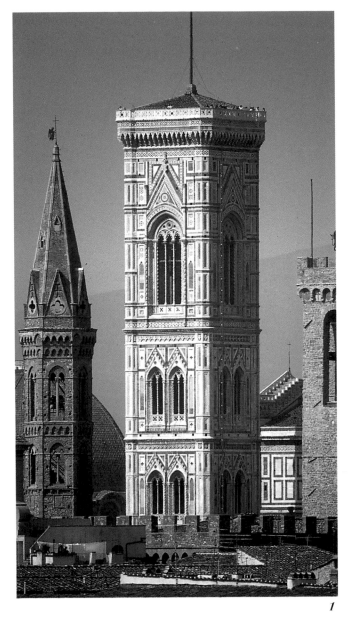

1

Charles the Fifth's troops entered the city in 1530 as victors. The Republic of Florence was vanquished. Among those who fought against the imperial forces in defence of the city and her republican government was Michelangelo. His rule was that of "military engineer". Despite this, Clement the Seventh requested that he remain in Florence and finish his work decorating the Medici Chapels. When the Medici Pope died in 1534 Michelangelo fled from his beloved city and went to Rome. He lived there for the rest of his life (1564). In 1530 the government rule was placed in the hands of Alessandro of the Medici, called "Moro," or the "dark-skinned". He was married to Margherita, daughter of Charles the Fifth, and in this way the plans of Pope Clement the Seventh were consolidated. The Pope was able to assure the political stability of the city allying the family with other powers. He arranged the marriage of Catherine of the Medici, great-granddaughter of Lorenzo il Magnifico, to Henry the Second, King of France. Cosimo (of the second branch of the family) followed Alessandro who was murdered by his cousin

Lorenzino in 1537. Cosimo was most clever in maintaining the delicate balance between Florence and other European nations such as France and Spain, following the teachings of the great political philosopher Machiavelli. Cosimo was also responsible for spreading the influence of power of the Medici, conquering the last of the Tuscan city states, Siena, in 1555. He then unified the region as the Grandduchy of Tuscany (1569). Thus begun a new period of splendour for the city and the Medici family. Francesco the First, who followed Cosimo, died early in his rule in the Villa at Poggio a Caiano. This was one of the most beautiful of the numerous Medici villas constructed on the hillsides surrounding the city. Florence was embellished in this period with magnificent structures such as the Forte del Belvedere, work of Bernardo Buontalenti and the Uffizi by Vasari. Other architectural masterpieces include the palaces built a few years earlier belonging to the powerful Pitti, Rucellai and Strozzi families. The Medici with the successors of Francesco the First no longer had the economic and, above all, political power of past generations. Their artistic and cultural interests remain, however, and eventually consolidated in the collections of the world renowned Gallery of the Uffizi and the Gallery of the Pitti Palace. In Florence a new form of musical

2

On the facing page: 1. Giotto's Bell Tower, the tower of the Florentine Abbey and the tower of the Bargello. 2. The Medici villa of Poggio a Caiano by Giuliano Sangallo. 3. The complex of the Medici Chapels.

3

Guelfan Palace

View including the Bargello and the Florentine Abbey

expression also had its beginnings, in the following centuries it is called destined to enormous success; called the melodramma, better known as the "opera". The Medici were not only patrons of art but also of the sciences. Under the protection of Cosimo the Second and Ferdinand the Second lived the astronomer from Pisa, Galileo Galilei. In his search for truth, he proved the empirical method as a necessary part of scientific methodology. His discovery and formulation of the laws of motion are the basis of all modern engineering, including space-craft. The fortune and power of the Medici began to fade with the last two Granddukes, Cosimo the Third and Giangastone. With the death of Anna Maria Ludovica, sister of Giangastone, the family line was extinguished forever (1743). The reign of the Grandduchy of Tuscany passed over to the Austrian House of Lorraine. These Princes knew how to win over the Florentine people especially due to their respect for the patrimony passed down by the Medici. The superb collections were further enriched. With a brief interruption corresponding to the Napoleonic domination, the House of Lorraine governed Florence until 1859. In this year the Grandduke of Tuscany, Leopold the Second, left Florence peacefully to its Italian destiny: unification. In 1860 the Kingdom of Italy was declared;

Florence was the capital from 1865-1871. In the city, in the second half of the 1800's, a new school of painting was established called the "Macchiaioli". Its greatest exponent was the Livornese Giovanni Fattori. It is similar in style to French Impressionism. Despite the dangers and destruction of World War II, the artistic and cultural identity of Florence - so profoundly rooted in the people and the monuments - is still intact. The population today is c. 500,000 inhabitants. The fortune founded during the period of the "Comune" was through commerce and handicraft. Still today the most important economic and productive growth is based on the same activities together with the tourist industry. Florence continues to be an important cultural centre with special programs such as the Maggio Musicale Fiorentino and the Mostra dell'Artigianato (Artisans's Show). The city continues to revive glorious historical moments in such folklorist events as the popular "Calcio in Costume" (Soccer in 16th Century Costume) and "Lo Scoppio del Carro" (the Explosion of the Cart). In a number of recent architectural projects such as the city stadium and the new Church of the Autostrada one rediscovers the artistic tradition which has made — and still makes — Florence one of the most beautiful and celebrated cities in the world.

The Old Palace (Palazzo Vecchio)

The "Scoppio del Carro," a ceremony held every year on Easter day

A phase of a "Calcio in Costume" game

9

The Religious Centre

The religious centre is formed by the union of two squares: piazza San Giovanni (St. John Square) with the Baptistry, the Bishop's Palace and the 14th century Loggia del Bigallo; and piazza Duomo (Cathedrale Square) with Giotto's Belltower and the Cathedral as well as the Brotherhood of "Misericordia" (Mercy) and the Museum of the Cathedral Artifacts (Museo dell'Opera). It is the natural centre of the city where many streets and alleyways converge. From any one of these roads the visitor has a u-nique "shot" or glimpse of incomparable beauty: the magnificence of the Cathedral, the elegance of Giotto's Belltower and the harmony and classical character of the Baptistery, which still have the magical effect of capturing and captivating the spectator who is experiencing this for the first time. This square of structures, expression of the wealth, power and ambition of a city of trade but also of art and culture (which was the character of medieval Florence), has been the proper "vestibule" or entry to the city for centuries. It still fills the generations of Florentines who have followed with a deep sense of pride.

"Beautiful St. John"

Dedicated to St. John the Baptist, patron saint of Florence, the Baptistry is the oldest building in the city. In fact, most historians today agree that the building was probably originally a Roman structure dating back to the 5th century. The marble decoration is instead in Romanesque style from the 11th-12th centuries. At the beginning of the 13th century the antique apse was substituted with the "scarsella". The "Beautiful St. John," as Dante described the building (Dante was one of the illustrious citizens baptized here), is composed of much material from the ruins of other structures. One of the interesting features is the gallery that runs around the interior just below the dome called the "matroneo". From the Latin word "matrona," it was space reserved exclusive-

Aerial view of the religious cente from which some of the mainc streets branch out

ly for the women. The pavement is rich in marble decoration with intarsia (note the signs of the zodiac). Above, in the vault of the dome, admire the glittering mosaics from the 13th-14th centuries. The figures emergings in the rich mosaics are of the Christian world: just above the triumphal arch we recognize the Last Judgement scene with the imposing figure of Christ who is separating the blessed from the damned. The rest of the scenes are divided up into horizontal bands which — starting from the drum of the dome — deal with stories of St. John the Baptist, Christ, St. Joseph and Genesis. Lastly, there is a hierarchy of angels and an ornamental frieze.

1. The Baptistery seen from Giotto's Bell Tower 2. The Baptistery — Vincenzo Danti (1539-1576), bronze group placed on the upper part of the Southern Door 3. The interior of the Baptistery, to the right the tomb of the Anti-Papa Giovanni XXIII by Michelangelo and Donatello. 4. On the following page: mosaics from the Baptistery's dome

The Doors of the Baptistry

Of the three doors of the Baptistry, the oldest set are the southern doors by Andrea Pisano (which now constitute the entrance), dating back to the first half of the 14th century. In the 28 panels there are represented in relief stories of St. John the Baptist and the cardinal, and theological, Virtues. The other two sets of doors are the works of Lorenzo Ghiberti. The northern doors, his first set, were executed in 23 years from 1401 to 1424. They are also formed by 28 panels enclosed in quadrilobed frames of still Gothic tradition and represent New Testament stories: there are also the 4 Evangelists and Doctors of the church. Lastly, there are the eastern doors, Ghiberti's greatest masterpiece. Completed in 27 years from 1425 to 1452, they are a testimony of the will and ambition of the artist to reach a formal perfection never seen before. These doors are subdivided not into 28 but 10 panels without frames. They deal with 10 stories from the Old Testament. The style of Ghiberti was always considered moderate and never revolutionary like that of his rival, Brunelleschi. Here instead it is novel and more appropriate to the Renaissance taste considering his understanding of perspective composition and his use of realistic detail. There are also recollections of antiquity done with a splendour and elegance satisfying the contemporary cravings. Considering also the intricate chisel work highlighted by the gilding, the doors were so splendid that Michelangelo, 50 years later, defined them as worthy to be the "Gates of Paradise".

1. The door known as Ghiberti's "Paradise" showing stories from the Old Testament 2. The southern door by Andrea Pisano 3. The northern door by Ghiberti. On the following page: at the top — detail of the "Creation of Adam and Eve" panel; at the bottom — detail of the "Cain killing Abel" panel

1

2

3

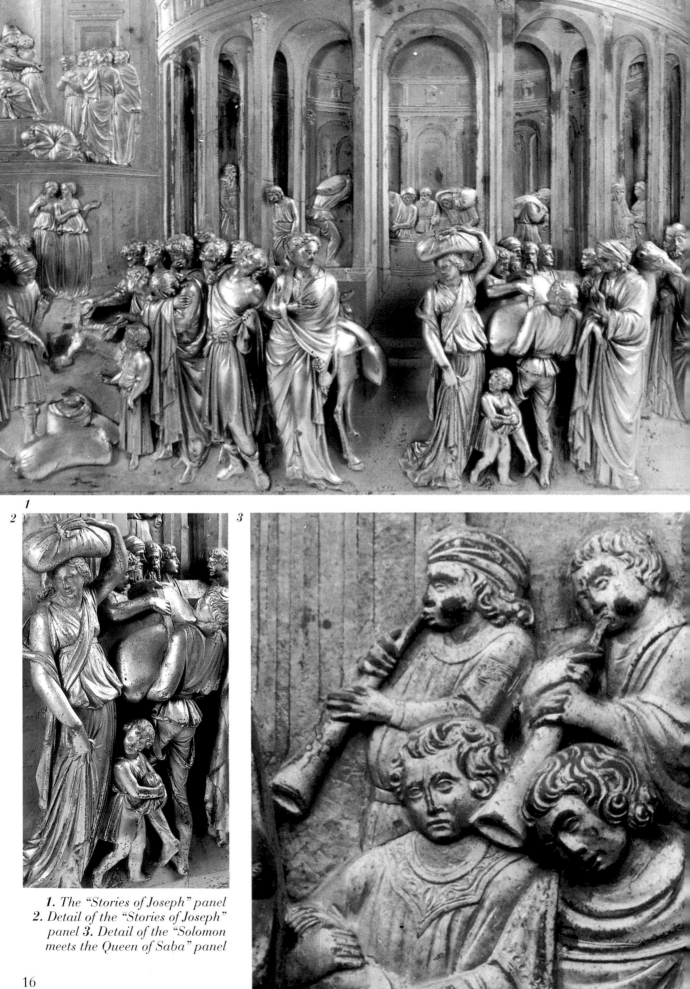

1. The "Stories of Joseph" panel
2. Detail of the "Stories of Joseph" panel 3. Detail of the "Solomon meets the Queen of Saba" panel

View of Piazza San Giovanni from Giotto's Bell Tower

The Cathedral

About 1296 it was decided that the ancient Cathedral dedicated to Santa Reparata (remains are visible in the excavations inside the Cathedral) was no longer suitable for a city of such dimensions and importance. It was Arnolfo di Cambio (who already one year earlier had begun the construction of the church of Santa Croce) who was commissioned the project for the new Cathedral named Saint Mary of the Flower. It is clear that the name was given in reference to the ancient Latin name of the city "Florentia" or "city of the flower". The works went on over a long period of time and only in 1436 — after 140 years — could Pope Eugenius IV consecrate the church. At the end of the 15th century the dome, or "cupola,"

was crowned with the lantern. Only at the end of the last century was the marble decoration of the façade completed according to the design of the architect Emilio de Fabris.
The interior - The church is in the form of a Latin cross with three naves separated by great pilasters and a choir from which extend the two lateral transepts and the semicircular apse. The austere appearance and extreme simplicity enhance the vastness of the ambience. Considering the length — 150 meters or c. 450 feet — this church is the 3rd largest of the Christian world after St. Peter's in Rome and St. Paul's in London. Fundamentally following the Gothic style, the massive cathedral maintains, however, a kind of moderation and a classical feeling that Florence had inherited directly from Rome. The

sharp contrasts and vertical reach characteristic of the Gothic are here restrained in the search for a composure based on the perfect square. The height of the central nave and the width of the church are each 38 meters in measure.
A place of many ceremonies and the memorable preachings of the Dominican monk Savonarola, the Cathedral was also the stage for the terrible assault called the "Pazzi Conspiracy". On Easter Sunday of 1478 assassins commissioned by Pope Sixtus IV and the Pazzi family tried to murder Lorenzo "il Magnifico" and his brother Giuliano of the Medici family. In the conspiracy, Giuliano was killed while his brother Lorenzo, with the help of friends, was able to save himself hiding in one of the sacristies of the church.

On the facing page: aerial view of the Cathedral. On this page: close-up of the Duomo's facade and Giotto's Bell Tower, with Palazzo Vecchio in the background

1

On the facing page: Cathedral — the 19th century facade by Emilio de Fabris. 1. Cathedral: interior 2. Domenico di Michelino: Dante outside of the walls of Florence, immersed in the worlds of his Comedy.

2

1. *Paolo Uccello: Equestrian monument by John Hawkwood.* 2. *Paolo Uccello: Clock from the interior facade of the Duomo. Executed in 1443; only during the last restoration was its original form recovered.* 3 - 4. *Details of the clock* 5. *Paolo Uccello: Glass window of the dome. On the following page:* 6 - 7. *The ancient Cathedral of S. Reparata, in the basement of the Duomo. Slabs of tombstones brought to light during the excavations after the flood of 1966.*

1

2

3

4

5

6

The Dome

Worthy of a separate chapter all to itself, the famous dome or "cupola" was constructed by Filippo Brunelleschi between 1420 and 1434. Of enormous dimensions — 45 meters in diameter and 114 meters in height — the dome was erected without the traditional use of scaffolding from the ground up. Brunelleschi employed a system using a double wall made of bricks laid herringbone fashion reinforced by a system of stone chains. The construction rose in circles ever smaller, ever tighter to the top. It was a double dome, with inner and outer shells; the architect left space in between for a stairway (463 steps) that rises up to the outdoor balcony around the lantern. The frescoes decorating the inner dome were begun in 1570 by Giorgio Vasari and finished after his death by Federico Zuccari. The stories represent the Last Judgement. At the beginning of the 1500's it was decided that the external drum of the dome be ornated with a bal-

7

cony in marble that went all the way around. The project was given to Baccio d'Agnolo who had finished the first of the eight sections in 1508. Having asked the opinion of the expert Michelangelo who described it as a "cage for insects," the authorities stopped the work.

1. The apse of the Duomo 2. Detail of the exterior of the Duomo towards the dome, seen from the Bell Tower. On the following page: Brunelleschi's Dome, with the latern made according to Brunelleschi's design in 1461 and completed with the copper ball by Verrocchio in 1474.

1

2

The Belltower

The plan of the belltower was designed by Giotto. He began the work in 1334 and carried it forth until his death in 1337. Andrea Pisano and, afterwords, Francesco Talenti continued the project, modifying the original design. Instead of the traditional peak or point, they completed the tower with a horizontal terrace.
Covered with polychromatic marble decoration, the 89-meter belltower was finished in 1359.

Museo dell'Opera del Duomo
(Museum of Cathedral Artifacts)

The museum was opened at the end of the last century when it was decided that works of art would be brought together, as well as displaced fragments of architecture and sculpture, from subsequently dismantled projects of the Cathedral, Baptistry and Belltower. From the last there are hexagonal panels with stories of the life of Man by Andrea Pisano and Luca della Robbia, and also 16 statues of prophets that were in the niches; among these, there are the famous "**Abacuc**" and "**Jeremia,**" sculpted with a bold realism by Donatello in 1436. From the Baptistry there is the silver altar as well as Donatello's "**Maddalena**," brought here after the most difficult restoration from damages caused by the flood of 1966. From the Cathedral, among other works, came the two "**cantorie**" or choir-lofts by Donatello and Luca della Robbia and the "**Pietà**" by Michelangelo. The choir-lofts are contemporary and date from 1431-1439. Comparing the two, the bal-

On this page: Giotto's Bell Tower. On the following page: 1. Works from the Duomo: choir-stalls by Donatello. 2. Works from the Duomo: "Madonna with Child" by Arnolfo di Cambio. 3. Works from the Duomo: Detail of the choir-stals by Luca della Robbia

2 3

1   2   3

1. Donatello: Magdalene, late work sculpted in wood; the last restoration enriched it with the original polychromatic coloring 2. Donatello: the prophet Abacuc, nicknamed "the Dunce" 3. Donatello: the prophet Jeremiah, nicknamed "Man of the People" On the following page: Michelangelo's "Pietà"

conies disclose the different currents developing in the Florentine Renaissance; they are two different interpretations of the classical ideal. Luca's style is more measured and pure; his figures move slowly in perfect harmony. Donatello's is more dynamic and alive where the little "putti" abandon themselves in an unbridled race under the "loggia".

The "Pietà"

Michelangelo was almost eighty years old when, for the third time, he chose the subject of the deposition. This "Pietà" was to be a part of his tomb and the artist sculpted his self-portrait in the hooded figure of Nicodemus. On the right is the Virgin whose face is almost disfigured in suffering; in the middle

Christ's body yields completely in death and, only with great effort, is supported by His Mother and Nicodemus. On the left is Mary Magdalene, sculpted later by Tiberio Calcagni. Michelangelo, dissatisfied with the quality of the marble, tried to destroy the work and left it unfinished.

The Medici's Neighbourhood

In just a few minutes from the religious centre one reaches the neighbourhood of San Lorenzo. It is a lively quarter of the city, the location of stalls making up the largest outdoor market in Florence. This neighbourhood was chosen at the end of the 1800's by the architect Giuseppe Mengoni for the most important architectural project of the 19th century, the "Mercato Centrale" or Central Market (indoor).
But San Lorenzo is above all the quarter of the Medici family.
According to the wishes of Cosimo, the great banker and head of the powerful family, their palace was constructed here and the church of San Lorenzo was rebuilt as well as the convent.
The tombs, instead, were decorated according to the desires of the granddukes.

The Medici Palace

Constructed in 1444 by Michelozzo, Cosimo's favourite architect, the Medici Palace is one of the most characteristic examples of civil architecture of the Renaissance. Massive and strong in its stone structure, the palace lightens in the upper floors where the broadness of the mullioned windows contributes a feeling of air and gives a refined quality to the structure. This was the residence of Cosimo the Elder, Piero, Lorenzo "il Magnifico" and all the court of men of letters and artists. With the advent of Cosimo I and the second branch of the Medici, the family moved into the Palazzo Vecchio (1540). Subsequently, the Riccardi Marquis acquired the palace (1655) and enlarged and altered the original form. Today it is the seat of the Prefect of Florence.

Interior - Admirable work in relief decorates the interior of the Baroque Gallery frescoed in 1682-83 by Luca Giordano (who painted in the vault the "Apotheosis of the Medici Dynasty") and also the Chapel frescoed by Benozzo Gozzoli with the "Procession of the Three Magi". Frescoed in 1460 under commission of Piero the Gouty, this "parade" recalls in the images represented a historical event of exceptional importance: the Ecumenical Council that Cosimo the Elder was able to bring from Ferrara to Florence in 1439. It was to be the last time the Churches of East and West would meet. Deserving admiration is the artist's attention to detail in meticulously painting the materials and embroidery of the costumes of Joseph, Patriarch of Constantinople, and of Emperor John Paleologus, as well as in depicting with exactness the prestigious members of the Medici family.

1. The "stalls" of the San Lorenzo Market. On the following page: 2. The Medici-Riccardi Palace by Michelozzo 3. The garden of the Medici-Riccardi Palace 4. Medici-Riccardi Chapel: Benozzo Gozzoli — detail of the "Procession of the Magi"

2

3

4

The Church of San Lorenzo

Founded in 393 by Sant'Ambrogio, the church of San Lorenzo was rebuilt in Romanesque style in the 11th century. The actual structure is a product of further rebuilding by Brunelleschi in the 15th century at the expense of the Medici family. More than a century later Pope Leo X commissioned Michelangelo with the project of the façade, but for lack of funds it was never done. The interior is of a unique purity. The harmony of the geometric lines and the rational equilibrium between the grey stone (pietra serena) and the white intonaco make this church one of the supreme examples of Renaissance architecture. In front of the main altar there is a plaque marking the place of burial of Cosimo the Elder of the Medici. This great honor was granted him by the Florentine citizens who elected Cosimo "Father of the Country" (Pater Patirae). The church is rich in works of art including two beautiful pulpits (late works by Donatello). At the ends of the transepts there are two sacristies: one is the work of Michelangelo and part of the Medici Chapels' museum; the other, on the left, is the Old Sacristy by Filippo Brunelleschi. Here too is revealed the style of the artist based on geometrical lucidity and equilibrium — nothing is left to chance, all is clear, calculated. The decoration is by Donatello; the large bronze sacrofagus (where Piero and Giovanni de' Medici, sons of Coismo the Elder, are buried) is an exquisite work by Andrea del Verrocchio (1472). From the left nave of the church, cutting across the end of the courtyard, one enters the vestibule of the Laurentian Library desigend by Michelangelo. The most impressive part of the decoration is, without a doubt, the stairway.

On the facing page: Benozzo Gozzoli — detail of the "Procession of the Magi". On this page: The Basilica of S Lorenzo

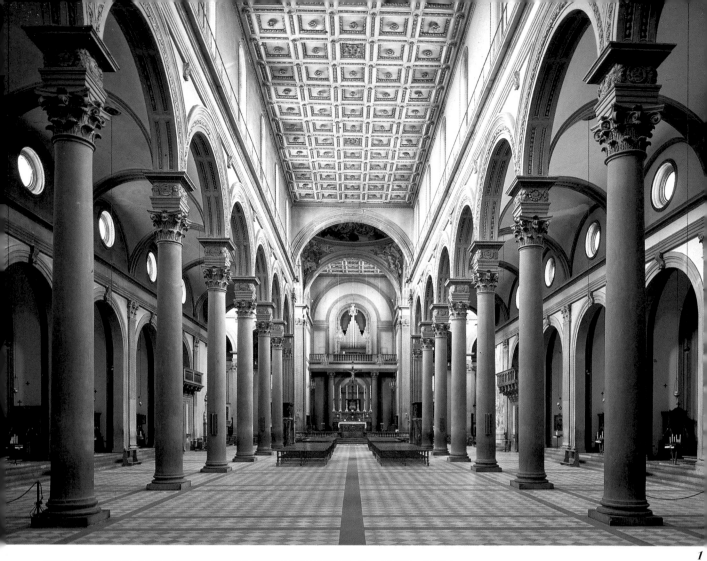

34

1

2

3

4

5

On the facing page: *1. Interior of the Basilica of San Lorenzo 2 - 3. Bronze pulpits by Donatello 4. The Old Sacristy 5. The Zodiac of the Old Sacristy with the celestial Hemisphere by Giuliano d'Arrigo, nicknamed "Pesello" 6. F. Lippi — "Annunciation" for the Martelli Chapel*

6

The Medici Chapels
The Sepulchre

As soon as one enters the vast crypt the meaning and function of the room are clear. Here are buried almost all of the Medici who belonged to the second branch of the family, the Grand dukes. Climbing a few stairs one reaches the **Chapel of the Princes**, an overwhelming and sumptuous Baroque interior begun in 1604 by Matteo Nigetti.

1. San Lorenzo, the staircase by Michelangelo in the vestibule of the Laurentian Library 2. The cloister of San Lorenzo 3. Aerial view of the San Lorenzo complex 4. Michelangelo: Madonna with child

1

2

It is embellished with marble decoration and the precious mosaic cre-
sts representing the cities of the
Grandduchy of Tuscany. The
school of the "pietra dura," or
"hard stones," was founded in the
16th century by the Medici and its
techniques are still used today. The
colours of the Florentine mosaics
are the natural hues of the marbles
and the semi-precious stones:
mother of pearl, lapislazuli, coral,
etc. The chapel was never completed. One sees, in fact, that the
niches above the enormous sarcophagi are all empty but two.
These two statues in gilded bronze
represent Ferdinand I and Cosimo
II by Ferdinando Tacca. The frescoes in the dome were added in
1826 by Pietro Benvenuti.

4

The New Sacristy

Commissioned in 1520 by Giulio de' Medici, later Pope Clemente VII, it was finished in 1534. It is one of Michelangelo's greatest achievements, in which he is responsible for both the architectural design and the sculptures. Here the drama of the opposing forces is expressed: that which is eternal and that which is finite in man.

The theme is that of man facing Eternity, represented in the four statues of nudes reclining on the two sarcophagi, symbolizing Day and Night on one side and Dawn and Dusk on the other. In the characterizations of Giuliano and Lorenzo, the figures sitting above the sarcophagi, the ways by which man might transcend the finite dimension of his existence are defined: through Heroism, admirably expressed in the boldness of Giuliano, Duke of Nemours; through Intelligence, apparent in the figure of Lorenzo, Duke of Urbino. But above all, that which saves man from the inexorable march of time is Faith; both Dukes are looking towards the Virgin Mary. In this chapel both Lorenzo "il Magnifico" and his brother Giuliano are buried. Their sarcophagus serves as base for the figure of the Virgin and the patron saints of the Medici, Cosmas and Damian.

These last two were sculpted by Giovanni Montorsoli and Raffaello da Montelupo. The architecture follows the motif of the Old Sacristy conceived by Brunelleschi a century earlier: a central plan based on the square surmounted with a dome

On the facing page: at the top, Chapel of the Princes (detail), decorated in hard stone and precious marbles; at the bottom: the octagonal dome with frescoes by Pietro Benvenuti. 1. Michelangelo — the sepulcher of Giuliano, Duke of Nemours 2. Michelangelo — the sepulcher of Lorenzo, Duke of Urbino. On the following pages: 1. Michelangelo: Night 2. Michelangelo: Day 3. Michelangelo: Dusk 4. Michelangelo: Dawn

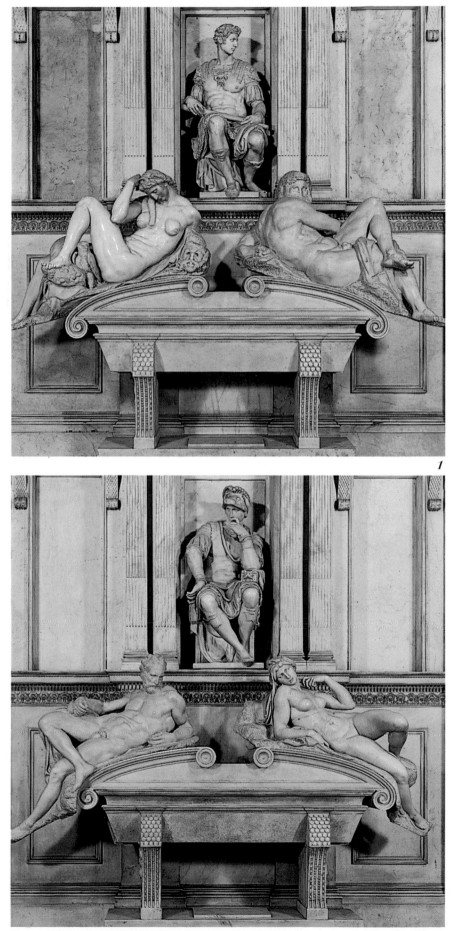

1

2

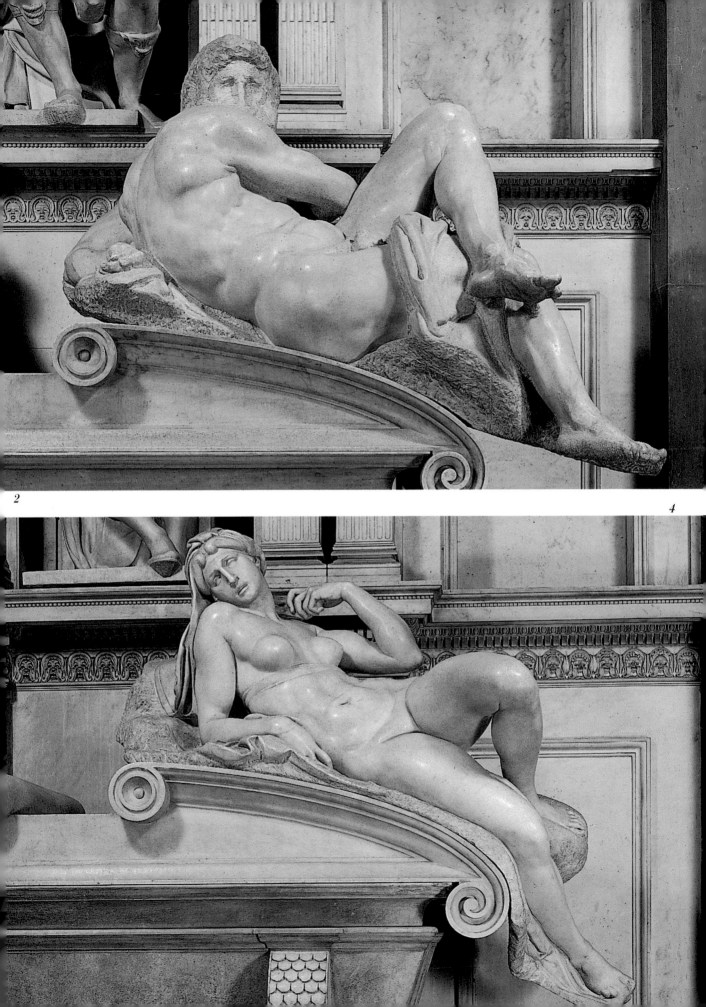

and decorated in gray stone on white intonaco. In Michelangelo however, the architecture is treated sculpturally: there is evident an increasing tension and greater force of the masses compared to the equilibrium and pureness of line of Brunelleschi. The space here has a less airy feeling and is more oppressed by the monumental quality that, in the coffered decorations of the dome, reminds one of the Pantheon of Rome.

The convent of St. Mark

Belonging to the Silvestrini monks until the 13th century, this convent was assigned to the Dominican brothers by Pope Eugenius IV in 1427. In 1437 Cosimo the Elder commissioned the architect Michelozzo to restore the convent and in a short time it became one of the most important centres of culture in Florence. Among the many illustrious figures who lived here St. Anthony, Archbishop of Florence, Girolamo Savonarola (with his doomsday sermons) and Beato Angelico are worthy of mention.
The latter's fresco work can be seen throughout the convent, so marvellously decorated from the cloister to the refectory, and all the way to the cells on the floor above. The convent was suppressed in 1866 and from that time on the building has been used as a museum. Dedicated to Beato Angelico, this is a classic example of a monographic museum where, among the frescoes and panel paintings, more than 100 works of the artist have been collected. The painting of Fra Angelico has been described as expression of a typically medieval religious inspiration, of a serene temperament that knows no disturbing or agitating elements. It is an expression born in a heavenly atmosphere perpetually inundated with light, whether it be glittering from the gold leaf of the divine space, or it be a clear, terse or diaphanous light of his landscapes. A man of the "holiest life" as Vasari describes him, Angelico, though profoundly moved by medieval spirituality, could not remain insensitive to the great arti-

stic innovations at hand — and all that was happening in Florence in the early 1400's outside the convent walls. This is how one explains the plastic and spatial aspects in his art that make him, without a doubt, a new artist, much closer to the spirit of Florentine Renaissance. In his artistic expression, above all, Church and World, Gothic and Renaissance, are indissolubly bonded together.

2

3

1. *Facade of St. Mark Church*
2. *B. Angelico: The "Universal Judgment". Detail of the "Elected". 3. B. Angelico: "Deposition". Executed for the Strozzi Chapel in the Santa Trinit Church c. 1433. It was begun by Lorenzo Monaco, and at his death in 1425 only the spires and the predella had been completed, now in the Academy Gallery. Angelico completed the altarpiece some years after.*

SALVE MATER PIETATIS ET TOTIUS TRINITATIS NOBILE TRICLINIUM
VIRGINIS INTACTE CUM VENERIS ANTE FIGURAM PRETEREUNDO CAVE NE SILEATUR AVE

1

On the facing page: above, Beato Angelico: Crucifixion with Saints (1441-1442); below, B. Angelico: Madonna on the throne with the Child among the Saint, known as the "Madonna of the Shadows" **1**. B. Angelico: Annunciation. One of the more noted compositions by the artist, executed between 1440 and 1450. **2**. B. Angelico: Institution of the Eucharist

2

B. Angelico: "Noli me Tangere," cell 1 — fresco

B. Angelico: "Nativity," cell 5 — fresco

B. Angelico: "Transfiguration," cell 6 — fresco

B. Angelico: "Jesus Derided," cell 7 — fresco

Piazza SS. Annunziata

This is one of the most beautiful squares of Florence with a feeling of harmony achieved by the three elegant porticoes that form the piazza: that of the church of the Annunziata, of the Confraternità dei Servi di Maria, and of the famous Ospedale degli Innocenti carried out by Brunelleschi in 1419-21. The façade of the "hospital" consists of a portico with 9 arches. The arches rest on fine and slender columns of the grey or "serene" stone and each is measured out in perfect regularity; the curve of each arch surmounts a square whose sides are formed by the columns. The medallions of swaddled infants in glazed terracotta by Andrea della Robbia (1487) have a beautiful decorative effect.

1. Piazza SS. Annunziata, the fontain of Pietro Tacca. 2. View of the Church of SS. Annunziata and the Hospital of the Innocents.

1

2

1

1. Basilica of the SS. Annunziata: interior 2. Pontormo: the Nazarene On the following page: Gallery of the Academy, Michelangelo's "David"

2

The Academy

Founded in 1784 by Grandduke Pietro Leopold, the Academy was enlarged and reorganized in the last century. In 1873 the architect Emilio de Fabris constructed the "Tribuna" purposefully to house the "David" by Michelangelo. Also by the artist one can admire the four "prisoners," the St. Matthew and the "Pietà of Palestrina" brought here in 1940.

The David

In 1501 the Florentine Republic commissioned Michelangelo with the figure of David. The artist was only 26 years old and at this time was firmly convinced of the theories of ideal beauty that had matured in the Neoplatonic Academy of the Medici court.
Beauty was understood as a reflection of the celestial world in this terrestrial one, almost a revelation of God; the human figure was the form in which divine beauty became most clearly manifest. He was also convinced that in order to reach a "superior" beauty he must search

1. *"David's" Tribune* **2.** *Detail of "David"*

and sift through nature, fantasy and idea. He did not believe, in fact, in the exact imitation of nature even if it fascinated him greatly. Michelangelo dedicated himself to the dissection of cadavers for the study of anatomy.

The result of these studies, theories and fantasies was the David, an ideal incarnation of this superior beauty, a work that is today one of the most well-known and admired in the world. Michelangelo took 3 years to finish this "colossus" of about 13.5 feet in height. In 1504 the statue was placed in front of the Palazzo Vecchio in Piazza della Signoria where it symbolized the liberty of the people of Florence and their will to defend it. The biblical hero is represented in the moment of greatest concentration, with the determined look of one who is ready to fight and who knows he must win. His moral force gives him an

2

expression of calm while his muscles reveal the inner tension manifest, above all, in the brusque movement of the neck. In his hands he holds the sling and the stone with which he will kill Goliath.

The Prisoners

These four statues were brought here from the "grotta" of Buontalenti in the Boboli gardens where the Grandduke Cosimo I had placed them. He had received the works as a gift after Michelangelo's death. They were originally to be a part of a grandiose project for the tomb of Pope Julius II, a project that Michelangelo was never able to finish and that was cause of profound disappointment and frustration for the artist. The statues are among the most perturbing ever sculpted, and what is most striking is the sense of oppression and the sign of struggle between the spirit and the material. In this very personalized style, the so called "non-finito" or "unfinished," one still sees the marks left by the chisel of the artist. Most of all we participate in the creative process and we are able to intuit the inspiration that accompanied the artist every time he was to undertake a new work. With just a little imagination it seems that inside these blocks of marble (just barely worked into), the figures are already modelled. Their force and beauty are such that we wait, fascinated and certain that they will slowly but surely liberate themselves. In the gallery there are also magnificent Flemish tapestries and a rich collection of paintings of the Florentine school of the 14th, 15th and 16th centuries.

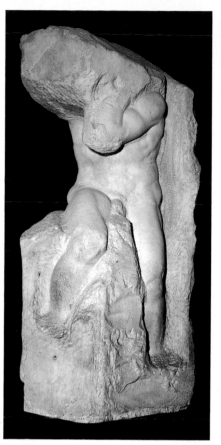

Atlantis

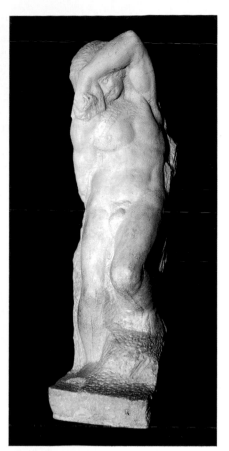

The Young Slave

The Bearded Slave

The Awakening Slave

1. Michelangelo: The "Pietà di Palestrina," made for the Barberini a Palestrina family 2. Michelangelo: Saint Matthew 3. Botticelli: Madonna with Child and Angels 4. Botticelli: Madonna of the Sea

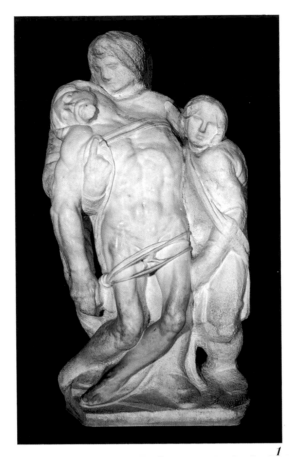

1

2

3

4

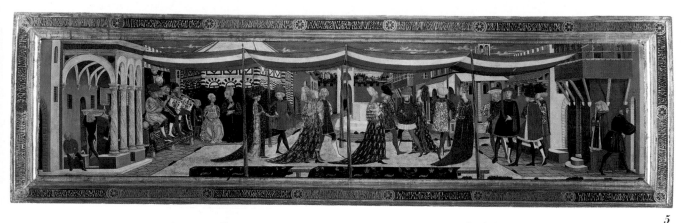

5. Adimari Chest 6. Pacino di Bonaguida: The Tree of Life

The Archeological Museum

Of fundamental importance for the study of Etruscan civilization and art, the archeological museum also includes Greek and Roman works, as well as an important Egyptian collection. The museum was founded in 1870 and is housed in a 17th century palace nicknamed "of the Little Cross". Amongst the most important works one can find: the CHIMERA WOUNDED BY BELLE-ROFONTE, Etruscan statue from the 5th century B.C.; a marvelous collection of bronzes discovered in Arezzo in 1555, whose restoration was executed by Cellini, among others; the ARRINGATORE ('her-ring fisherman'), another example of 3rd century B.C. Etruscan art; and — without doubt the most pre-cious piece in the museum — the ceramic FRANCOIS VASE from Ergotimos factory in Athens, execu-ted by the Greek artist Klitias in the 6th century B.C.

In this museum one can also admire Etruscan sarcophagi and ceramics as well.

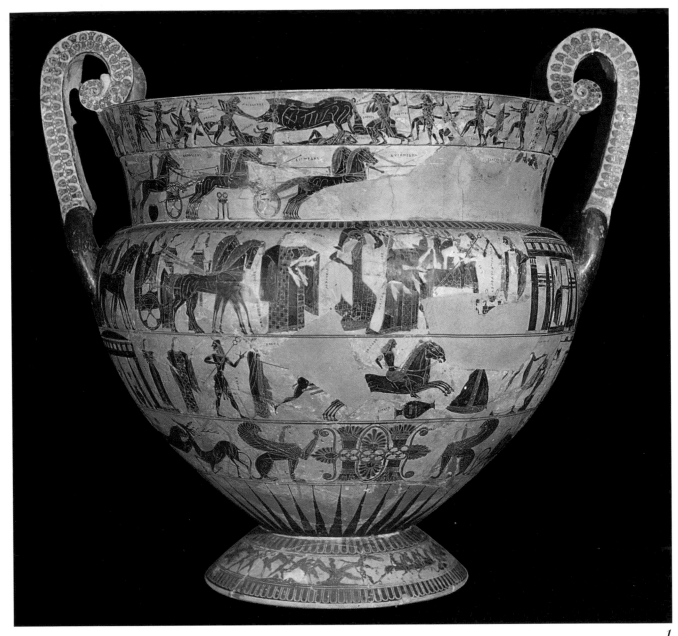

1

2

1. Archeological Museum: the Francois vase that was found in the last century and was acquired by the Grandduke Leopoldo II. 2. The garden of the Archeological Museum 3. Sarcophagus of Larthia Seianti, in terra-cotta with polychromatic decoration (Chiusi, 2nd century B.C.) 4. The Chimera, Etruscan bronze from the 5th - 4th century B.C. 5. Apollo Milani, Greek Kouros from the 6th century B.C.

3

4

5

The Synagogue

In the last century, after the destruction of the ghetto, the banker David Levi left available for the sum of 1,500,000 lire the construction of a new Jewish temple. The building was commissioned to three architects — Treves, Micheli and Falcini — and was finished in 1882, after about 8 years. Today the synagogue of Florence is considered one of the most beautiful of Europe and its characteristic moorish style is a reminder of the Spanish origins of the first Jewish community here. The contemporary community, after the Holocaust of the Second World War, has no more than 1,500 members. The war wreaked serious damage to the building, but even greater damage was wreaked by the flood of 1966 when many of the sacred books (Tora) were lost.

1- 2. The Synagogue: by the architects Treves, Micheli and Falcini, finished in 1882.

1

The English Cemetery

Along the avenues which encircle the city, halfway between the ancient northern gate (Porta San Gallo) and the eastern gate (Porta alla Croce), one finds the English cemetery where the famous poetess Elizabeth Barret Browning is buried (d. 1861). Prompted by social and especially political interest (the Italian Independence Wars), after marrying, she and Robert Browning settled permanently in Florence in the Casa Guidi. This house lent its name to the poem "Casa Guidi Windows," the most famous of her works inspired by the Italian Risorgimento.

2

The Central National Library

The project for the construction of a new national library was commissioned to the Roman architect Cesare Bazzani. The building was erected from 1911-1935 on the space once occupied by the old barracks. The library was the most damaged of the culturally pertinent buildings in the flood of 1966. Many volumes were saved from the mud thanks to the efforts of young people, Italian and foreign, whose admirable self-sacrifice will never be forgotten by the Florentines and the world. The library contains about 4,000,000 volumes and periodicals, 25,000 manuscripts and codices, 700,000 letters and documents and 15,000 maps.

The Russian Church

The outstanding monument of the Russian national art is located near Fortezza da Basso, on via Leone X, 8. The Orthodox church was built in 1899-1903 by means of the rich and aristocratic Russian Colony (one quarter of the sum was given by the Demidoff family). The author of the project M. Preobragensky had chosen the style of moscovite architecture of XVII century. The main cubic structure is topped by five domes, while the porch is covered by a "tent". Such Italian masters as architect G. Boccini, marble-carver G. Novi, casters Michelucci had taken part in the construction.

The edifice has two stories: the upper church is dedicated to the Nativity of Christ and the lower one is dedicated to St. Nicholas. The walls are entirely covered by paintings, based on scetches of Russian painters. The marble iconostasis was donated by the Tsar Nicholas II.

Santa Croce

St. Francis of Assisi, apostle to the poor, died in 1226 and was canonized in 1228. From that time his followers began to disperse throughout Italy and settled in the poorest neighbourhoods of the cities. There is evidence that in 1229 a church dedicated to the saint was constructed in Florence. It was on the ruins of this little church that Arnolfo di Cambio — in 1295, a particulary wealthy period in the city — began the construction of Santa Croce. The stained-glass windows give a luminosity to the interior which is designed in the form of an egyptian cross (T) of overwhelming dimensions. This is the largest Franciscan Church in Italy. The church was subject time and time again to "restoration"; unfortunately, in the second half of the 1500's much of the original decoration was destroyed. Andrea Orcagna's frescoes were practically "erased" and substituted on the walls with heavy altars by Vasari. The style of the church is Gothic, but not heavy and austere like that of the Cathedral. The pilasters, in fact, are more slender. the ceiling is not cross-vaulted but constructed with enormous painted wood beams and the walls are much thinner. Today Santa Croce represents a place of sacred memories for the Italians and has become a kind of "Pantheon" of the city where c. 300 men of great importance for letters, music, science, art and politics are buried. With time the church has been enriched with famous works of art; among them there is the marvellous PULPIT by Benedetto da Maiano (c. 1472) with five bas relief panels of the life of St. Francis in amazing perspective. There is also the "ANNUNCIATION" by Donatello in grey, or "serene," and gilded stone dating from c. 1435. The funeral monuments or TOMBS of the humanists Leonardo Bruni and Carlo Marsuppini were executed by Bernardo Rossellino and Desiderio da Settignano, respectively. These two tombs are tabernacles surmounted by an arch and enclose a sarcophagus with a funeral bed above. This plan became the pro-

1. Basilica of S. Croce. View of the Piazza. 2. Basilica of S. Croce 3. Interior of the Basilica of S. Croce 4. Benedetto da Maiano: Pulpit with stories of Saint Francis

1

2

3

4

1

2

3

totype of the Renaissance tomb. At first glance they seem very similar to each other. Stylistically speaking, however, one notes how the severe monumental quality and equilibrium of Bernardo's design is in contrast to the purity, softness and refined elegance of Desiderio's tomb. There are also the FRESCOES of the chapels near the apse, two of which, the Bardi Chapel and the Peruzzi, are superb late works by Giotto. In the Bardi Chapel Giotto presents again — after the Assisi frescoes 30 years earlier — the stories of St. Francis. There are six narrative episodes. Of these the death of the saint stands out most impressively; one is struck by the intensity of the scene, the expression and the participation of every figure. The way in which the character of each individual monk has been portrayed is extraordinary.

On the facing page: Interior of the Basilica: the Apse 1. The Annunciation by Donatello, in "serene" stone 2 - 3. Detail of the "Annunciation"

1

2

The Tombs of the Great

Tomb of Michelangelo Buonarroti, 1475-1564

Michelangelo died in Rome in February of 1564 at the age of 89. The project for the tomb dates back before his death and is by Vasari, who placed at the top — above the sarcophagus — the bust of the artist. At the base of the monument there are the three allegorical figures of Painting, Sculpture and Architecture.

Tomb of Niccolò Macchiavelli, 1469-1527

"Words are not enough to praise" says the Latin inscription on the base, one of the finest ever written. Niccolò Machiavelli, secretary of the Florentine Republic at the beginning of the 16th century, was fundamentally a politician and in his book "The Prince" he characterized himself as believer in the politics in which "the ends justify the means". The funereal monument, executed by Innocenzo Spinazzi, dates from the end of the 18th century and presents at the top the allegorical figure of Diplomacy.

3

Tomb of Galileo, 1564-1642

Born in Pisa the same year that Michelangelo died, Galileo lived almost his entire life in Florence where he found in the Medici court the trust, admiration and means necessary to carry on his revolutionary studies of the motion of Earth. The monument with the allegorical figures of geometry and astronomy was designed by Giulio Foggini. Among the many tombs note those of other illustrious figures: GIOACHINO ROSSINI, VITTORIO ALFIERI, LORENZO GHIBERTI, UGO FOSCOLO, etc., as well as the cenotaph in memory of DANTE ALIGHIERI (buried in Ravenna).

1. Michelangelo's tomb, by Vasari 2. Machiavelli's tomb, by I. Spinozzi 3. Galileo Galilei's tomb, by G. Foggini 4. The Bardi Chapel: Giotto. The apparition to Brother Agostino and the Bishop — detail. 5. Bardi Chapel: Giotto — The Death of Saint Francis

4

5

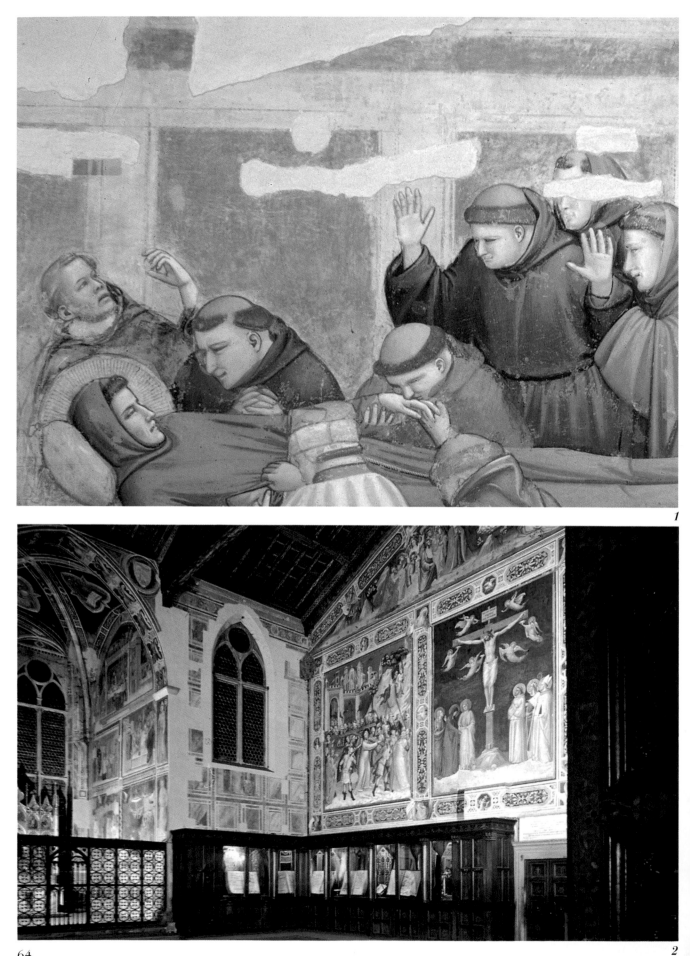

1

2

1. Giotto — Detail of the death of Saint Francis 2. Rinuccini Sacristy and Chapel 3. Baroncelli Chapel 4. Panel of the "Crowning of the Virgin" by Donatello 5 - 6. Details of the frescoes in the Baroncelli Chapel

The Pazzi Chapel

In the picturesque cloister to the side of the church of Santa Croce one finds one of the greatest works by Filippo Brunelleschi: the Pazzi Chapel. It dates from just three years before the death of the architect (1443). The plan of the chapel is again the circle and the square. A rectangular base is covered with a conical central dome supported by fine "veiled" vaulting that one also finds in the porch. The spaces are divided up with a geometric lucidity; the white intonaco of the walls is in cool contrast to the pilasters in grey "serene" stone, and the beautiful decorations in glazed terracotta which adorn the interior are by Luca della Robbia. In the same courtyard there is the long refectory housing the dramatic CRUCIFIX by Cimabue. Dating from c. 1270 this was the work of art most damaged in the flood of 1966. Ten years time was necessary for the restoration of the panel painting. After lying immersed in the mud for an entire day, it seemed irredeemably lost.

1

2

3

4

1. F. Brunelleschi: cloisters with the Pazzi Chapel 2. View from above of the first cloister 3 - 4 - 5. F.Brunelleschi: Evangelists 6. Cimabue: Crucifix, before the flood of 1966 7. Large refectory, on the right the Crucifx by Cimabue after the flood of 1966.

5

6

The Buonarroti House

Bought by Michelangelo for his nephew Leonardo, the "Casa Buonarroti" today houses an interesting museum. Apart from early works such as the *Battle of the Centaurs*, the bas relief of the *Madonna of the Stairs* and the wooden *CRUCIFIX* from the church of Santo Spirito, the museum is rich with sketches, studies for architectural projects, and personal letters of the artist. There are also commemorative paintings of the artist's life done by his grand-nephew Michelangelo the Younger. The museum-house is just a few minutes walk from the church of Santa Croce.

1. Detail of the "Madonna of the Stairs" 2. The Battle of the Centaurs

1

2

Bargello

Built in 1255, this is the city's first town hall or "Palazzo del Popolo". It was the seat of the "Captain of the People" until 1261 and then became the seat of the "Podestà," or elected magistrate, who represented the people and was the most important person of the Republic. The mandate of every Podestà was never a Florentine; his term lasted only one year so that he might not become too familiar with the private affairs of the citizens. In this way he was impartial and incorruptible, and law could be rigidly enforced. On the walls of the courtyard one can still see the coat of arms of various Podestà from over three centuries. In the 16th century, with the fall of the Republic and the beginning of Medici rule, the Duke instituted a special corps to maintain order in the city. The head of this "corps" was the Captain of Justice, or "Bargello," and the pa-

Bargello: exterior with the Volognona tower, realized in 1250 for the Captain of the People by Lapo Tedesco

1 3

2

4

5

1. Bargello: courtyard 2. The Hall of Verrocchio 3. The Hall of '300 4. The Balcony 5. Ammanati: Leda 6. Michelangelo: The "Tondo Pitti"

lace named after him became his residence from 1574. Towards the end of the 1700's, thanks to the House of Lorraine, capital punishment was abolished and all the torture instruments were burned here in the courtyard. Lastly, in 1860, the Provisional Government of Tuscany allotted the structure as a National Museum. The ponderous structure built on the side of the tower called the "Volognona" is cube-shaped and is crenellated with Guelph-style battlements. The courtyard is particularly evocative and is bordered on three sides by heavy rounded arches which support the upper loggia and floors. There are on display one of the richest collections of Renaissance sculpture as well as innumerable examples of the "minor arts" such as ceramics, ivories, enamels, etc.

6

The Tondo Pitti dates from c. 1505 when Michelangelo was 30 years old. United with the artist's personal and innovative style there is still the tradition of Donatello, especially in the "schiacciato," or "flattening," of little St. John in the background.

Baccus is one of Michelangelo's earliest works (1497) still clearly based on classical theme and form. It is simply stunning the way the artist rendered the feeling of precarious equilibrium and instability in the inebriated youth.

The Apollonian David by Michelangelo can be related to the Prisoners of the Academy and dates from 1530. It is a statue alive with contrast: the left shoulder is pulled back while the right juts forward; one leg is behind while the other is forward. It seems as if he is turning and only maintains his equilibrium because of the rhythm of these contrasting motions.

The two panels with the SACRIFICE OF ISAAC date back to 1401, executed by Ghiberti and Brunelleschi for the competition of the construction and decoration of the Baptistery doors. After a dispute among the judges, the commission was given to Ghiberti. Undoubtably we are dealing with two distinct personalities. Brunelleschi, new man of the Renaissance, eliminates

1

4

5

6

much decoration and many classical allusions and, without delay, immerges himself in the drama of the event. His vision is original and his modelling hard. Lorenzo Ghiberti is, instead, an admirer of beautiful forms; he loves to evoke the classics and he lingers on innumerous details. His scene is more restrained, the soul of the characters calmer. It is interesting to compare the two Isaacs. Brunelleschi's Isaacs is more alive, more veritable. He doesn't want to die and in the moment when the angel holds back Abrahams's hand, the muscles of his legs are still taut, strained, as if he wants to flee. Instead Ghiberti's Isaac does not react; it is as if he offers himself in sacrifice, with pride and disdain flaunting the beauty and classical perfection of his body.

Brutus (c. 1540) - In the Renaissance the figure of Brutus was equated to a hero who sacrifices his dearest sentiments for the liberty of his country. Michelangelo accepted this interpretation and exalted Brutus with the greatest vital force. With his head turning unexpectedly

to the side, he has the proud and resolute look of one who has performed a noble deed.

Donatello - Equal to Brunelleschi, Donatello was also a new man of the Renaissance, the greatest sculptor of the early 1400's. He was a

1. Michelangelo: David-Apollo 2. L. Ghiberti: panel with the sacrifice of Isaac 3. F. Brunelleschi: panel with the sacrifice of Isaac 4. Michelangelo: Brutus 5. B.Cellini: Cosimo I 6. A. Della Robbia: Madonna of the Cushion

master who, opposing the academic tendencies to see only the classical as model, wanted to affirm his own realism in his quest to capture the essence of his personalities, the individuality of his figures.

The Bargello offers a vast selection from his artistic production: from the powerful plasticism of his ST. GEORGE sculpted in 1416 for the church of Orsanmichele, to the bronze DAVID of 1430 executed on commission of Cosimo the Elder and which represents the first nude of the Renaissance.

There are also: the playful and carefree putto called ATHIS; the vigorous and commanding NICOLÒ DA UZZANO, bust in polychromatic terracotta; and also the thin and fragile figure of ST. JOHN executed for the Casa Martelli.

73

1

2

3

4

5

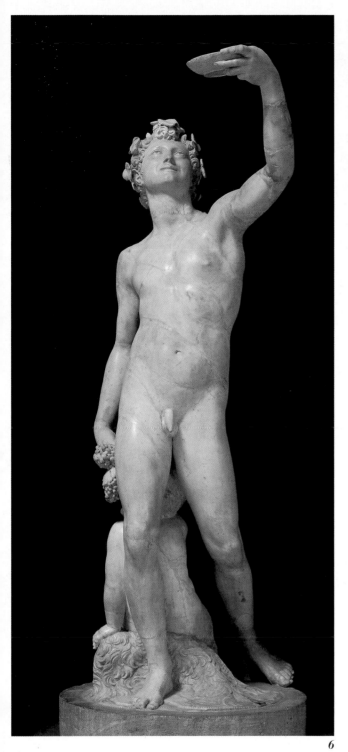

6

7

Besides Donatello's sculptures the museum offers a panorama of the greatest masters of the 1400's and 1500's, from the forceful characterization of mostly Florentine personalities (such as the marble busts by Antonio Rossellino, Mino da Fiesole, Pollaiolo and Benedetto da Maiano), to the delicate and graceful image of the *Woman with the Little Bunch of Flowers* by Verrocchio. Here is a play of light: it is falling, settling on and highlighting her face and the sheer gauze of her dress, down to her very fine hands. Considering the sculptor's sensibility to light, some claim there is the influence — if not the direct collaboration — of his young pupil Leonardo da Vinci. Also by Verrocchio is the bronze DAVID which has been compared many times to Donatello's and which seems to be less aware of the great feat he has performed. Perhaps Verrocchio had wanted to refrain from a search for profound meaning in his work and instead was concentrating his efforts on a vivacity and a nonchalance in his young, bold hero. There are many other works on display as well: the MADONNA WITH CHILD by Luca and Andrea della Robbia, other bronze and marble masterpieces by Cellini, Giambologna, Laurana and Bernini, etc.

Orsanmichele

Built in the first half of the 1300's by the architects Francesco Talenti, Benci di Cione and Neri di Fioravante, this church of an unusual square shape was originally a loggia utilized as a grain market; towards the end of the 1300's the arches of the loggia were closed and two upper floors were built. The 14 niches on the exterior walls contain statues of patron saints of the various guilds, or corporations, of work. Donatello, Ghiberti, Nanni di Banco, Verrocchio and Giambologna are among the artists who sculpted or fused in bronze the statues. Inside the church there are the celebrated TABERNACLE by Andrea Orcagna (1349-59), worked so intricately in polychromatic marble and stained glass, and the panel painting of the MADONNA OF THE GRACES inside the Gothic tabernacle attributed to the Florentine artist Bernardo Daddi (1347).

1

2

1. View from Orsanmichele from Palazzo Vecchio 2. Church of Orsanmichele: Tabernacle of the Orcagna 3. Robbian tondo attributed to L. Della Robbia 4. The "Little Pig" by Pietro Tacca 5. The Loggia of the New Market, nicknamed the Market of the "Little Pig"

3

4

The Political Centre
Piazza della Signoria

Centre of the political and social life of the city for centuries, it is without a doubt the most beautiful square of Florence, built upon the ruins of the Ghibelline homes of the 13th century. The square's name actually derives from the PALACE where already in the 14th century the government of the Republic (called the "SIGNORIA") resided. This structure — still today the seat of the Comune and of the offices of the Mayor — dominates the entire square which is "crowned" with beautiful statues and appears to the visitor a genuine "open-air" museum. The piazza has been the stage of innumerable historic events: from the riots of the 1300's to the solemn ceremonies and proclamations of the Medici; from the execution of those who had conspired against Lorenzo and Giuliano in 1478 (when the bodies of the murderers dangled from the windows of the palace) to the assassination of Savonarola.

After being tortured on the rack for weeks in the palace, this Dominican monk was hung and burned along with two other brothers on the 23rd of May, 1948. One can read about this dramatic incident in the round, marble plaque in the pavement in front of the Neptune fountain. The nearness of this square to the museums and principal monuments of the city have made it a meeting

On this page: Piazza della Signoria; on the following page: the "Biancone" by Ammannati

place for all. At the end of an intense and tiring day, one can sit at a table at one of the outdoor cafés and enjoy the "show" at sunset: the stones of the Palazzo Vecchio become honey-coloured and seem to give off a soft glow while the statues are already in the shadows.

The "Loggia"

The famous 14th century Loggia "of the Lanzi" or, more commonly, "of Orcagna" to whom the construction has been attributed, rises on the same side of the piazza as the palace. A number of sculptures are on display under the elegant arches of the loggia which were erected between 1376-1382 for the public ceremonies of the Signoria. First, there are the six Roman statues against the wall in back representing heroines. There is also the RAPE OF POLISSENA, a 19th century work by Pio Fedi. HERCULES AND THE CENTAUR is by Giambologna. To the sides of the loggia there are two masterpieces: PERSEUS WITH THE HEAD OF MEDUSA by Benvenuto Cellini and the RAPE OF THE SABINES by Giambologna. Cellini was considered the finest Florentine goldsmith of the 1500's and his school became a tradition. Still today there are many Florentine goldsmiths' workshops. The Perseus was cast in bronze from 1545-1554. For the execution of the work Cellini had to overcome a number of problems for the fusion. In the end the work was a perfect success and Cellini was capable of exhibiting anatomical and decorative detail in this outstanding statue. The "Rape of the Sabines" dates to 1583 and is one of the most admired and enjoyed of this Flemish artist, Giambologna. In the twisting and intertwining of the three figures, the exceptional technical ability of the artist is manifest. This sculptor lived many years in the court of the Medici.

The Other Statues of the Piazza

On the steps of the palace, at the sides of the entrance, there are the statues of HERCULES AND CACCUS, by Baccio Bandinelli, and a copy of David that in the last century replaced the original by Michelangelo. Both the Hercules and the David were placed in front of the Palazzo della Signoria as a symbol of the liberty won, jealously guarded by the Florentines. They were also a symbolic warning or challenge to whomever might have tried to take over the Republic. On the corner of the palace there is the famous figure of NEPTUNE in white Carrara marble. It is a work by the artist who undoubtably had more success as an architect than as a sculptor: Bartolomeo Ammannati. The fauns and the marine divinities are works fused in bronze by Giambologna, who is also responsable for the impressive equestrian monument of Cosimo I, Grandduke of Tuscany of the Medici family.

The Palace

The construction of the Palace was begun in 1298, presumably according to the design of Arnolfo di Cambio. Characterized by the rustic

On the facing page: Piazza della Signoria: the Loggia of the Lanzi 1. Giambologna: the Rape of the Sabine 2. Cellini: Perseus

"bugnato" (rough hewn stone), the palace has always been a visible affirmation of the power of the Comune that it represented. From the embattlements jutting upwards from the base soars the fortified tower — 94 meters high — named after Arnolfo. It is certainly an audacious architectural solution capable of expressing the boldness and uniqueness of the entire structure. One can see above the great clock at the base of the tower the

window of the "Alberghetto" which was a cell in the 15th century for the imprisonment of Cosimo the Elder and Savonarola. Below the arches of the balustrade of the body of the building there are numerous coats of arms representing political entities of the Comune of Florence. For ten years, from 1540 to 1550, it was the residence of the Grand-duke Cosimo I; then the Medici moved to Palazzo Pitti.

From that time on the building was

1

On the facing page: Palazzo Vecchio
1. Detail of Palazzo Vecchio, the
clock and the municipal coat of
arms 2. Palazzo Vecchio:
the courtyard by Michelozzo

called the Palazzo Vecchio or "Old Palace". When Florence became capital of Italy the palace was chosen as the seat of the Chamber of Deputies and for the Ministry of Foreign Affairs. Lastly, since 1872, it has been the seat of the Comune of Florence.

The Courtyard

This is a 15th century work by the architect Michelozzo. It sustained restoration and alteration in the 16th century when Vasari, on the occasion of the wedding of Princess Joan of Austria to Cosimo's first son Francesco, frescoed the walls with scenes of Austrian cities. In the centre of the courtyard there is a playful and gracious fountain with a winged putto in bronze. It is a copy of the original by Verrocchio, visible inside the palace.

2

The Great Hall of the 500

Built in 1494 by Simone del Pollaiolo nicknamed "Cronaca," this room of impressive dimensions (53 x 22 m) had the purpose of hosting the General Council of the People in the time when the Medici were in exile and the city was governed by a Republic.

When the Medici returned after the siege of 1530, Vasari was in charge of renewing the room's decoration. He had the ceiling raised to a height of 18 meters and he designed for it a pictorial scheme.

There are 39 compartments illustrating events from Florentine history and allegories based on the life of Cosimo I. He placed in the very center the triumph of the Grandduke.

Then he proceeded to decorate the walls where a number of years earlier Leonardo da Vinci and Michelangelo contended in the execution of enormous frescoes (unfortunately lost) featuring the Battle of Anghiari and the battle of Cascina. Here, too, in the frescoes Vasari narrates the conquests of Tuscan provinces by the Medici.

Around the room there are the LABOURS OF HERCULES, 16th century sculptures by Vincenzo de' Rossi and the VICTOR by Michelangelo. This sculpture was originally meant for the tomb of Pope Julius II and it is the only work which remained in Michelangelo's studio until his death.

The sculpture symbolizes classical beauty in the young nude who poses with one knee resting on the back of the bearded prisoner he has subdued. From a little door in the great hall one enters the "STUDIOLO of Francesco I" created in 1570 by Vasari. He built the rectangular room with barrel vaulting and had it decorated on all sides. Looking down on the scheme from the lunettes are the portraits by Bronzino that Francesco wanted of his parents, Cosimo and Eleonora.

1

2

3

4

5

4

5

1. Vasari: the conquest of Porto Ercole, detail 2. Vasari: the siege of Livorno, detail 3. Vasari and Stradano: the siege of Florence (Clemente VII's room) 4. The "studiolo" of Francesco I 5. Donatello: Judith and Olofernes (Hall of the Lilies)

The Second Floor

Climbing the stairs on the right, one enters the "Quartiere degli Elementi," or the "Apartment of the Elements," with rooms enriched with frescoes by Vasari and others presenting mythological subjects. There is also the Apartment of the Grandduchess Eleonora, daughter Viceroy of Naples don Pedro di Toledo and wife of Cosimo I. Among the most interesting rooms note the Sala dell'Udienza (Audience Room) with its magnificent coffered ceiling by Benedetto da Maiano and frescoes by Francesco Salviati (1550) which narrate, in mannerist style, stories of Cammillo. The bronze statue of JUDITH WITH THE HEAD OF HOOLOFERNES is a late work by Donatello and was just recently moved here from the Piazza della Signoria for protection from the "elements" that it suffered from for nearly 5 centuries.

Also worth seeing are the Sala dei Gigli named after the decoration of lilies on the walls and the Sala delle Mappe, or "Guardaroba".

In this room, on the carved doors of the cupboards, there are 53 geographical maps of the second half of the 1500's by Ignazio Danti and Stefano Buonsignori.

On the facing page: at the top, the Hall of the Lilies; at the bottom, the Priòri Chapel. On this page: at the top, the Hall of Leo X; at the bottom, the Green Room.

The Uffizi

The palace dates back to 1560 when Vasari was commissioned to build a structure that would house the offices of the city government — thus the name Uffizi from the word "uffici," or "offices". The palace has a superbly scenographic setting: it is inserted in the political centre between the Palazzo Vecchio and the river with marvellous "shots," or "angles". For example, standing under the arch of the shortest block of the structure on the bank of the Arno, one can focus in on Arnolfo's tower of the Palazzo Vecchio and all the sculptures lined up in front of it. The material used for the building is, once again, the traditional "pietra serena," or grey stone, in contrast with the white intonaco. In 1581 Francesco I managed to expropriate rooms from the burocracy and created the famous gallery on the top floor. He collected in the rooms of the Tribune some paintings and outstanding sculptures continuing the great cultural heritage that characterized his successors, as well as the House of Lorraine (the Austrian Granddukes of Florence). Because of their interest in collecting art forms, the Uffizi became one of the most complete art galleries of Italy and one of the most outstanding of the world. Along the two principal corridors there are 45 rooms where the celebrated paintings are displayed in chronological order. Starting with the first room, one may have a comprehensive visit following the development of the various schools (above all, the Florentine school from the 13th to the 17th century). The corridors themselves are richly embellished with the finest tapestries of both Flemish and Florentine schools of the 16th century, as well as Roman statues and sarcophagi.

The Enthroned Madonna by Cimabue - Cimabue has unanimously been considered the first great maestro in painting and therefore the initiator of the Florentine school. This altarpiece comes from the church of Santa Trinità and was painted at the end of the 13th century. Differing from the Byzantine paintings that presented only two

1

2

dimensions, width and height, the Madonna by Cimabue is enclosed here in a space that can already be defined as "in perspective". The throne itself curves back giving a feeling of depth. (Note the beautiful "cosmatesque work," the decoration on the throne still of byzantine style). Below, the four prophets pose in precise, well-defined spaces.

Giotto's "Maestà" - By tradition considered a pupil of Cimabue, Giotto executed the Maestà in 1310 for the church of Ognissanti.
These are among the prominent characteristics of his style: monumentality, a plastic quality, a greater characterization of his figures who are finally free to express their sentiments or emotions, and a rendering of perspective.

Madonna with St. Anne - This is a work that Masaccio and Masolino painted together, dating from c. 1423. Masaccio is responsible for the Virgin and Child, as well as the angel in green in the upper middle right. To the still Gothic refinement of Masolino, the younger Masaccio opposes with a sense of volume and solidity in the forms. In the distribution of light and shade, and the system of perspective construction, many critics have defined him as "Giotto reborn".

The Battle of San Romano - The Uffizi Gallery possesses only one of the three paintings on wood that Paolo Uccello executed around 1456 depicting an episode of the victorious battle of the Florentines against Siena.
The other two works are in the Louvre in Paris and the National Gallery in London. The composition presents figures crushed one against the other and is extremely

On the facing page: View of the Piazzale of the Uffizi 1. Cimabue: Maestà of S. Trinità 2. Giotto: Maestà of Ognissanti

appealing in the fantastic use of colour (note the horses), as well as the diverse points of perspective which seem to force all the figures up front and render the entire scene immobile, static and surreal.

1

2

3

Madonna with Child - Filippo Lippi - Datable to around 1465, it is a late work and among the best known of the Carmelite brother Filippo Lippi. Like many of his contemporaries, Lippi's career began with the study of the frescoes by Masaccio in the Carmine church. His style, however, breaks with Masaccio's in his use of fine lines to give a gracefulness, sweetness and sensuality to the figures.

Federico da Montefeltro - This masterpiece is by Piero della Francesca, one of the greatest artists of the 1400's whose activity was mostly centred in Urbino. This portrait is of paramount importance for the aerial perspective of the background and for the meticulous detail work of Flemish influence in the description of the features of the Duke of Urbino.

1. Simone Martini: The Annunciation 2. Masaccio and Masolino: Sant'Anna Metterza 3. F. Lippi: Madonna with Child and Angels 4 - 5. Piero della Francesca: the Dukes of Urbino 6. Paolo Uccello: the Battle of S. Romano

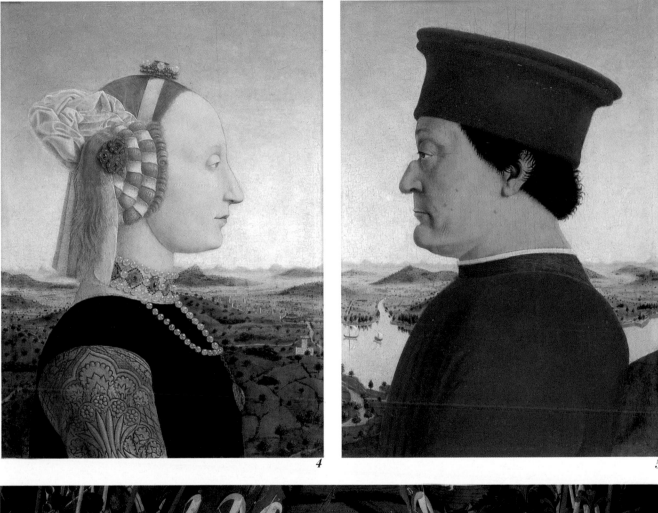

4   5

6

Botticelli: Madonna of the Melagrana. On the following page: at the top, Botticelli: "Spring"; at the bottom, Botticelli "The Birth of Venus"

Botticelli - His career began in the school of Fra Filippo Lippi, but early on his aristocratic style captured the attention of the Medici. Botticelli lived and worked many years at the court of the Lords of Florence. Because of his fine sensibility he was able to translate into images the contemporary neo Platonic philosophy of Lorenzo "il Magnifico" and the scholars of the court. He was fond of allegories (thus the conflicting interpretations of the PRIMAVERA) and his work, so pregnant with a bittersweetness and melancholy, is almost never composed in a realistic manner. His visions are those of a dreamer; his compositions are not unified or centrally focused. On the contrary, one must read them by shifting the eyes, following the lines which seem to flow with a soft, musical rhythm.

1

2

3

4

1. Botticelli: Madonna of the Magnificat 2. Gentile da Fabriano: Adoration of the Magi 3 - 4. Venus of the Medici, Helenistic copy from the original of the 4th century B.C. 5. The Tribune 6. Leonardo: The Annunciation

The "Tribuna" - Designed by Bernardo Buontalenti in 1585, this beautiful octagonal room held the masterpieces brought here by Francesco I and which constituted the beginning of the Uffizi Gallery. Although disrobed of some of those works, the room is still richly decorated: in the middle there is a splendid table in Florentine mosaic; all around some of the finest classical sculptures are on display, among which there stands out the famous **Medici Venus** (3rd century B.C.). On the walls there are a number of portraits of the Medici, for the most part in Mannerist style. Bronzino's portrait representing Eleonora from Toledo is most striking.

Leonardo da Vinci - Averse to the neoPlatonic philosophy of the Court of the Medici, Leonardo was instead

5

1

2

a lover and student of nature, whose variations and mutations he rigorously depicted in minute detail.

He left, in fact, the refined atmosphere of Florence when still young. Unfortunately, the Uffizi does not possess much of Leonardo's artistic production; the only works present are the ANNUNCIATION and the ADORATION OF THE MAGI. Leonardo painted the former when he was only 23, and it already discloses the values of the artist's work in his career. They are: a meticulous description of nature (such as the representation of the wings of the angel, the tree of the landscape and the flowers of the garden); a careful study of atmosphere with a particular interest in twilight. The tonal effects in the play of light and shade at sunset fascinated Leonardo so much as to encourage the artist to develop a new technique in painting. This was far removed from the more typical "chiaroscuro" and is called "sfumato," or "smokey". He was commissioned "The Adoration of the Magi" by the brothers of S. Donato at

3

Scopeto in 1482, and left it unfinished due to his departure for Milan. Here is a very personal interpretation of the subject bound up in complex figure patterns, in tension and in the portrayal of human emotion.

Leo X - Raphael - This masterpiece painted by Raphael shortly before his premature death is of a great coloristic intensity. Giovanni dei Medici became Pope Leo X and is represented here as an assertive and successful man, a man who dominates his world.

Madonna of the Goldfinch - This celebrated Madonna is an early work by the artist. Contrary to the portrait of Leo X, it is more typical of the 1400's in style. The group is composed in a pyramid shape and formed by the Virgin, St. John the Baptist and Christ in front of a sublime landscape background that gradually dissolves in the depths. The figures are simple and depicted with an equilibrium and calm typical of this artist's "language".

The Tondo Doni - The subject of the painting is the Holy Family and was executed c. 1504 by Michelangelo on the occasion of the wedding of Maddalena Strozzi and Agnolo Doni. Once more the artist emphasizes the modelling of the bodies and the movement of the figures. The group is compact and solid, almost as if they were sculpted from one block of marble. As if inside a glass sphere, the Virgin twists and turns on her own axis and her projection heightens the

1. Raphael: portrait of Leo X 2. Raphael: Madonna of the Goldfinch 3. Leonardo: Adoration of the Magi 4. Michelangelo: Sacred Family (Doni Tondo)

4

feeling of volume. Like many
Mannerist artists, Michelangelo
chose cold colours in light - dark
tones.

The Venus of Urbino - Titian -
This is one of the many paintings
by Titian which came from Urbino
and became a part of the Medici
collection when Ferdinand II married Vittoria della Rovere. It is a
masterpiece of Titian's mature
period dating from around 1530.
The composition is rich in warm
tones which serve the artist to
express the pleasures and sensuality
of this palpable and natural beauty.

*1. Rosso Fiorentino: Angiolo
Musicante 2. H. Van der Goes:
Portinari triptych.On the following
page: at the top, Tiziano: "Venus of
Urbino"; at the bottom, Canaletto:
view of the Ducal Palace of Venice*

2

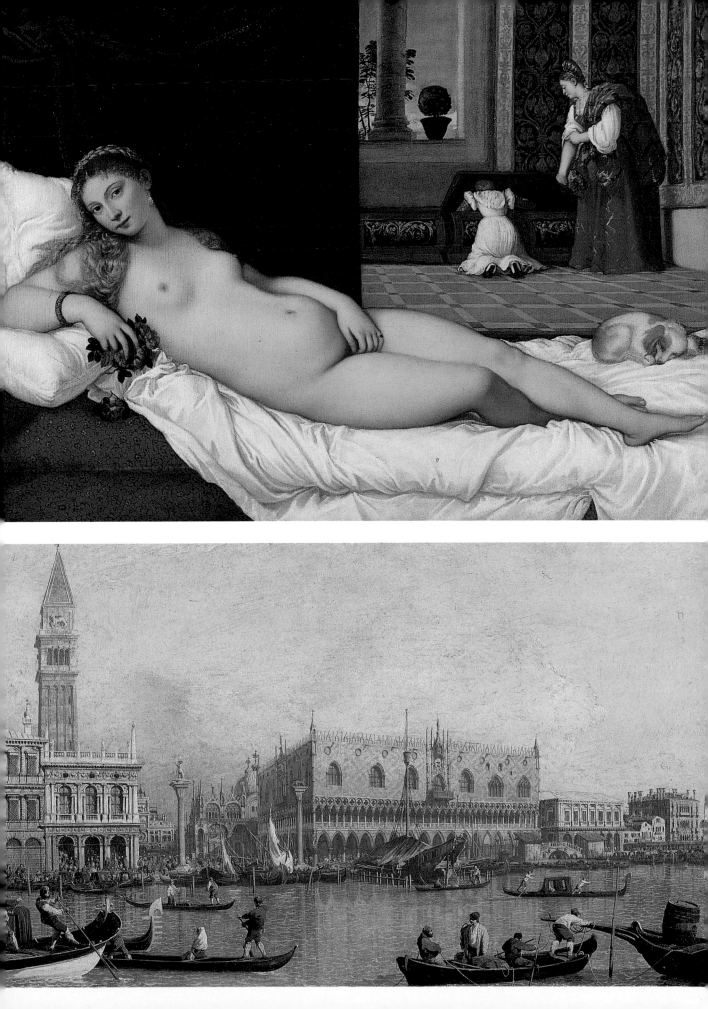

The Old Bridge

This unique bridge crosses the Arno where the river bed is narrowest. It is the oldest bridge of Florence and the only to survive intact the mines of the Nazis in WW II. The first wooden bridges were destroyed again and again due to the flooding of the Arno. Finally this more resilient bridge was constructed in stone in 1345 by Neri di Fioravante. Under the Medici in the 1500's it was reserved for the goldsmiths who opened their shops, still famous the world over.

The Vasari Corridor

When the Medici family moved over to the Pitti Palace, Giorgio Vasari was commissioned to construct a corridor that linked the Grandduke's new residence to the city's administrative offices in the Uffizi and the Palazzo Vecchio. Crossing over the goldsmiths' workshops of the Old Bridge, this hallway was finished c. 1565 and is about one kilometre in length. Today it is most famous for the collection of paintings that decorate it. They are mostly self-portraits of artists of all periods. There are wonderful views from the windows.

On these two pages: images of Ponte Vecchio, attributed to Neri di Fioravanti (1348), which unites, via the Vasari Corridor, Palazzo Vecchio and Pitti Palace

Santa Maria Novella

This is the first monastic church of Florence. Belonging to the Dominicans, the church dates from 1278 when two brothers of the order, Fra Sisto and Fra Ristoro, began the construction. In 1470 the architect Leon Battista Alberti completed the beautiful façade of the medieval church in polychromatic marble. The innovative design in the façade of the side volutes gives it a unique quality and harmony; it is considered one of the outstanding façades of the Renaissance. The interior is elegant and graceful in Gothic style. Particularly interesting and impressive is the sense of depth given by the convergence of the pilasters whose distance between one another decreases as one approaches the high altar. Among the many works of art in the church, the frescoes by Ghirlandaio are noteworthy, painted from 1485-1490, decorating the entire choir behind the main altar. The stories are narrated in a pleasing manner and concern the lives of Mary and St. John The Baptist. In the left nave is the very famous TRINITÀ fresco by Masaccio from 1427. On the side of the church is the convent where one finds, to the left of the entrance, the CHIOSTRO VERDE or "green collister". Walking through, one reaches the Sala Capitolare or CAPPELLONE DEGLI SPAGNOLI (Spanish Chapel). This rectangular room from 1350 was designated in the 16th century by Eleonora da Toledo for the religious functions of the Spanish of her court. The vaults and the walls were frescoed in 1355 by Andrea di Buonaiuto. Note the grand wall paintings or frescoes on the sides representing the "Militant Church" and the triumph of the Dominican Order and the "Triumph of St. Thomas of Aquine".

1. The Church of S. Maria Novella begun on an antique oratory in 1246. 2. The interior of the Basilica, realized by Vasari as well 3. Ghirlandaio: apparition of the Angel to Zacchary 4. Masaccio: the Trinity 5. G. della Robbia: Washbasin of the Sacristy

3

1

2

4

5

1

2

3

4

5

6

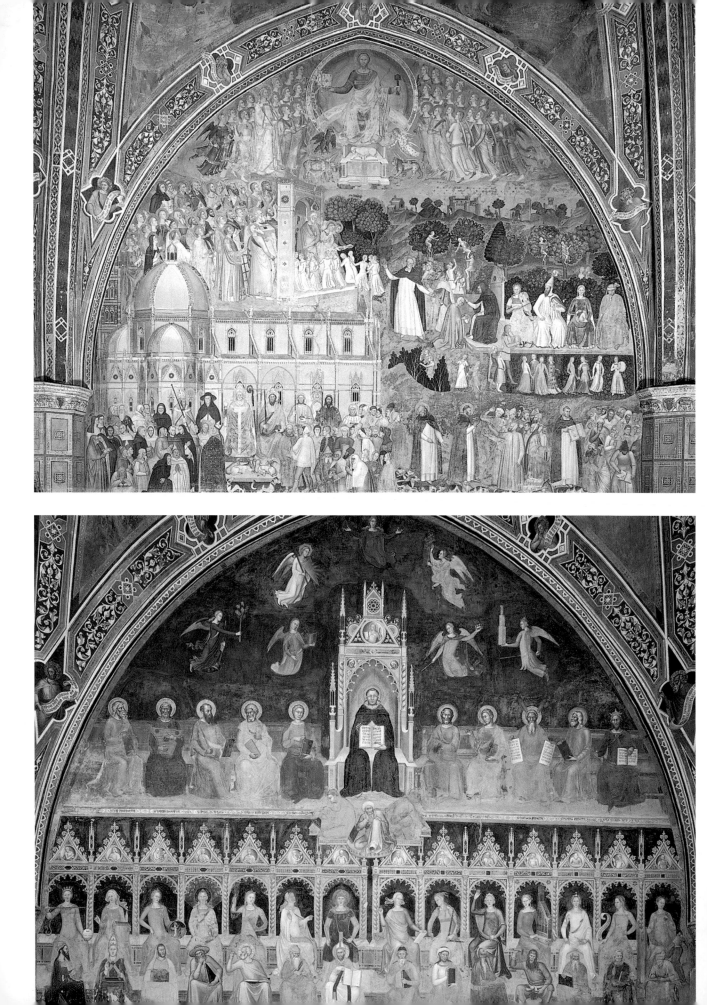

Palazzo Pitti

According to legend Luca Pitti, Florentine banker and rival of Cosimo the Elder, had commissioned the architect Brunelleschi to construct a palace that had windows as large as the Medici's doors and a courtyard as large as the entire Medici palace.

Work began in 1458 after the death of Brunelleschi but was shortly stopped due to the economic ruin of the family. In this way Eleonora da Toledo was able to buy the structure in 1549 and had the building enlarged and embellished.

The palace was still further enlarged in the 17th century and towards the end of the 18th century the front wings, called "Rondò," were added on. Considering its 205-meter length, Palazzo Pitti is the most prodigious of the city.

Residence of the Medici Granddukes until the death of the last member in 1743, it became then the home of the Austrian House of Lorraine. After the proclamation of the United Kingdom of Italy and the transfer of the capital to Florence (1865-1871), the palace became the official residence of the King of Italy Victor Emmanuel II and the House of Savoy.

Today the palace belongs to the state and boasts a number of outstanding museums and galleries: the Palatine Gallery, Museum of Silverworks and Vases, the Museum of Modern Art and others.

The Boboli Gardens

On the same hill behind the palace extend the Boboli Gardens, a most typical example of an Italian-style garden. Designed by the architect Tribolo, the gardens date from the 16th century and were truly a work of "green architecture" where the Medici might enjoy their sumptuous

1. Pitti Palace: facade
2. Boboli Gardens: basin of the Islet
On the facing page: Spanish Chapel (Cappellone degli Spagnoli): above Allegory of the Church. Below Triumph of Saint Thomas.

1. Pitti Palace: view from the Boboli Gardens
2. Valerio Cioli: statue of the dwarf Morgante,
nicknamed "Bacchus"
3. Staircase of Boboli Gardens

The Former Royal Apartments

These rooms were originally inhabited by the Medici and the Lorraine. When Florence was capital (1865-1870), King Victor Emmanuel II remodelled and refurnished them as receiving, or audience, rooms for entertainment. They are richly decorated with furniture and objects of art, tapestries, mosaics and paintings. Particularly interesting are: the "Room of the Niches," or dining room (Sala da Pranzo), the Throne Room with precious Chinese and Japanese vases, as well as the canopy with the Savoyard coat of arms; and the grand Ball Room (the "White Room"), finely decorated with stucco in neoclassical style. This room is now used for special exhibitions and concerts.

*Apartments: **1.** The Throne Room*
*   **2.** The Queen's Room*

1

2

The Palatine Gallery

Differing from the Uffizi, the rich collection of paintings in the Palatine Gallery are not on display in chronological order. Instead of abiding by scientific museum criterion, all has been left according to the taste of the princely court. The initiator of this collection of paintings was Cosimo II. During the 17th century the upper part of the walls and the ceiling vaults were decorated in Baroque style by Pietro da Cortona and Ciro Ferri.

On this page, Raphael: "Madonna of the Chair" of 1515. With a smile full of grace and gratification, this Madonna appears extremely different to us than that painted by Raphael during the Florentine period. The dignifed movement of the figures inside the tondo of the frame confers harmony to the composition, while the extreme refinement of the mantle and the use of changing colors reveal the influence of Venetian painting.

On the following page: Raphael: the "Veiled Woman," or the "Fornarina," of 1516. Here the relationship to the countryside vanishes in the background. The geometry dominating the composition makes the portrait more monumental and sets the spectator at direct contact with the beautiful character wrapped up in the veil.

1

2

1 - 2. Raphael: Agnolo and Magdalene Doni, painted c. 1506. That of Magdalene is most famous because of certain matchings with the "Monnalisa" by Leonardo, painted few months before, and because of the relationship between the figure and the still Perugina-like Umbrian background.
3. F. Lippi: Madonna with Child
4. Raphael: Madonna with Child, nicknamed "Of the Grandduke": This is the first of the masterpieces from that phase of Raphael's art which experienced an ever increa-sing influence from Leonardo.
5. Murillo: Madonna with Child
6. Rubens: The Consequences of the War, an allegory from 1638 painted in Anvers and sent to Florence where it was acquired by Giusto Susterman, court painter of the Medici family.

3

4

5

6

1. Titian: Magdelene, executed between 1530 and 1540: it is the expression of those chromatic values with which the Venetian school — and in particular Titian — competed against intellectual classicism, based on Tuscan designs. 2. Titian: Portrait of a Gentleman, another wonderful example of Titian's portraiture (c. 1540). 3. Ruysch: Flowers, Fruit and Insects

1

2

3

Church of Santo Spirito: Facade.

The Churches of the "Oltrarno"
(other side of the Arno river)

Between Palazzo Pitti and the Ponte Vecchio stands a little church dedicated to the Roman martyr "Santa Felicità". Crossing above the portico of the church is the Vasari Corridor that opens up onto the interior with a balcony so that the granddukes could assist in the mass even from above.

This church possesses one of the masterpieces of the Florentine Mannerist period of the early 1500's: the "Deposition," painted by Pontormo in 1527. Far from any traditional plans, there is no background here and the figures are virtually weightless as if suspended in air. The high emotional pitch, the drama and the use of exquisite irridecent colors in this deposition from the Cross, have contributed to make it justly considered Pontormo's greatest work. In the centre of the characteristic and popular neighbourhood of San Frediano rises the church of Santo Spirito. This is the

Church of Santo Spirito: Interior.

most important of the churches of the Oltrarno, a late work of the architect Brunelleschi (1444). It has undergone remodelling in subsequent centuries. The smooth and simple façade dates from the 18th century.

*1. Pontormo: Deposition.
Church of S. Felicità*

1

Masaccio in the Carmine Church

In this church, in the Brancacci Chapel, there is the most important fresco cycle of the 1400's: the stories of San Pietro painted, for the most part, by Masaccio with great vigour and sobriety. The artist was working here from 1425-28. The modelling given to the forms, the individualization and the definition of character of the figures, as well as the perfect geometric perspective of the scenes, have served as the school for all of the artists of the Renaissance, including the great Michelangelo. Below: THE TRIBUTE MONEY - It is the most famous and monumental scene of the cycle. The expression of St. Peter is of great intensity. He is indomitable and inflexible in his faith. The scene describes in three phases an episode narrated in the Gospel of St. Matthew. In the centre the tax collector asks Christ for the tax and He, with a decisive and controlled gesture, indicates to St. Peter where he will find this money. The scene shifts to the left where St. Peter

2

3

4

5

takes the money from the mouth of a fish; on the right, he pays the tax collector. Masaccio's sensitivity is evident in the reaction of St. Peter who receives the order. By intuition he has perceived the miracle and imitates Christ's gesture.

2. *View of the Carmine Church*
3. *Interior of the Carmine Church*
4. *Brancacci Chapel*
5. *Masaccio: the Tribute*
6. *Masaccio: the Tribute — detail*

6

1

2

3

4

5

1 - 2. Masaccio: the Tribute —
detail 3. Masaccio: the Tribute
— detail 3. Masaccio: the
Expulsion of Adam and Eve
4. Piazza S. Trinità
5. Church of S. Trinità: interior
6. Ghirlandaio: Church of
S. Trinità — Sassetti Chapel,
the Adoration of the Pastors

6

121

1

2

San Miniato

This church, dedicated to the first and only Florentine martyr, is one of the finest examples of a Romanesque structure and dates back to the 11th century. The position of the church, is extraordinary; standing in front of the church, one dominates the entire city and the panorama is simply superb. Perhaps just as impressive: while walking along the Arno at night, one looks up to see the illuminated façade of San Miniato; the reflection of light on the green and white marbles and mosaic has often been compared to an intricately decorated jewelry box. The church is composed of three naves and a presbytery where, in the apse, there is a fine mosaic of the 13th century. The ceiling is of wood beams, the ancient system of covering the basilicas or Paleo-Christian churches. Noteworthy in the interior: the integration of the Florentine Romanesque with the 15th century Renaissance in the tabernacle by Michelozzo, situated in the central nave below the presbytery.

1. View of the Basilica of S. Miniato on the Mount 2. Interior of the Basilica 3. Pulpit from the Florentine school of the 13th C. 4. Mosaic — Jesus Christ, the Virgin and Saint Miniato 5. Spinello Aretino: Saint Benedict receives King Toptila 6. Spinello Aretino: the Death of Saint Benedict

3

4

5

6

1

2 3

4

1. *Piazza della Repubblica*
2. *Strozzi Palace* 3. *Church of the Crate* 4. *S. Trinità Bridge* 5. *The Ognissanti Church* 6. *The Carthusian Monastery of Galluzzo, general view*

5

6

1

2

Fiesole

Situated on the top of the northern hill of the same name, 300 meters above sea level, Fiesole, the city of Etruscan origin, is the best known town in the Florentine vicinity.

Of notable historic and artistic importance, the city safeguards works of art and monuments such as the ROMAN AMPHITHEA-TER from the first century B.C. Only brought to light at the beginning of the last century by the archaeologist Friedman von Shellershein, it has a seating capacity of 3,000 people.

3

4

5

6

7

*1. Aerial view of Fiesole 2. The hills
of Fiesole seen from S. Domenico
3. The Church of Saint Francis
4. The Cloister of Saint Bernard
in the Convent of Saint Francis
5. Remains of the archeological
zone, Roman Theater 6. The
Bell Tower of the Duomo in Fiesole
7. Facade — the Abbey of Fiesole*

INDEX

© ATS Italia Editrice S.r.l. – Made in Italy
www.atsitalia.it
email: atsitalia@atsitalia.it
Rome: Via di Brava 41/43 – tel. 06 66415961
Florence: Largo Liverani 12/3 – tel. 055 4220577

The trademark Ŝ is a trademark of ATS Italia Editrice

© Photographs:
ATS Italia Editrice S.r.l.
References:
ATS Italia Editrice S.r.l., Gaetano Barone, Stefano Cellai, Patrizio Del Duca, Gianni Pasquini, Scala S.p.A., Kina Italia, Sergio Cipriani, K e B News, Press Photo, Nicola Grifoni, Arte e Immagini S.r.l.

Test: Riccardo Nesti
Graphic design and layout: Carlo Mannucci
Editing: ATS Italia Editrice S.r.l.
Translations: International Service, Sandra Fanti, Olga Federova, Mikhail Talalay
Composition: Leadercomp, Stampa Nazionale
Photo reproduction: Studiolito 69
Printing: Kina Italia / L.E.G.O.